PIANO SOLO

Y0-BZF-956

Disney · PIXAR
FINDING DORY

ISBN 978-1-4950-7314-4

**Wonderland Music Company, Inc. /
Pixar Music
Sis 'N Bro Music Company obo
Unforgettable Standards [U.S.A. Only]
Bourne Co. [Rest of the World]**

© 2016 Disney Enterprises, Inc./Pixar
Disney/Pixar elements © Disney/Pixar

DISTRIBUTED BY

7777 W. BLUEMOUND RD. P.O. BOX 13819 MILWAUKEE, WI 53213

For all works contained herein:
Unauthorized copying, arranging, adapting, recording, Internet posting, public performance,
or other distribution of the printed music in this publication is an infringement of copyright.
Infringers are liable under the law.

KELPCAKE

Music by
THOMAS NEWMAN

© 2016 Wonderland Music Company, Inc. and Pixar Music
All Rights Reserved. Used by Permission.

FINDING DORY
(Main Title)

Music by
THOMAS NEWMAN

© 2016 Wonderland Music Company, Inc. and Pixar Music
All Rights Reserved. Used by Permission.

JEWEL OF MORRO BAY

Music by
THOMAS NEWMAN

© 2016 Wonderland Music Company, Inc. and Pixar Music
All Rights Reserved. Used by Permission.

Moderately slow, freely

Moderately, evenly

GNARLY CHOP

Music by
THOMAS NEWMAN

Moderately fast

© 2016 Wonderland Music Company, Inc. and Pixar Music
All Rights Reserved. Used by Permission.

ALL ALONE

Music by
THOMAS NEWMAN

© 2016 Wonderland Music Company, Inc. and Pixar Music
All Rights Reserved. Used by Permission.

JOKER AT WORK

Music by
THOMAS NEWMAN

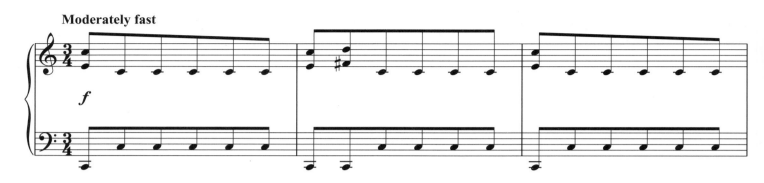

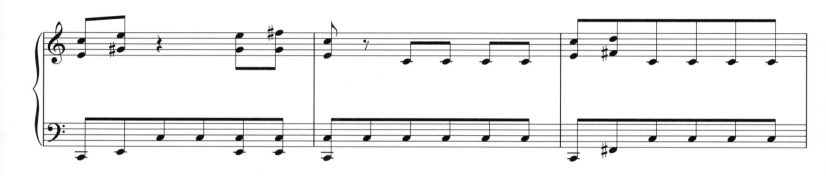

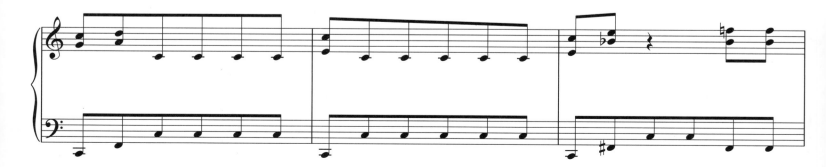

© 2016 Wonderland Music Company, Inc. and Pixar Music
All Rights Reserved. Used by Permission.

ALMOST HOME

Music by
THOMAS NEWMAN

© 2016 Wonderland Music Company, Inc. and Pixar Music
All Rights Reserved. Used by Permission.

...SHELLS

Music by
THOMAS NEWMAN

© 2016 Wonderland Music Company, Inc. and Pixar Music
All Rights Reserved. Used by Permission.

21

Moderately

Pedal ad lib. to end

rit.

a tempo

OKAY WITH CRAZY

Music by
THOMAS NEWMAN

© 2016 Wonderland Music Company, Inc. and Pixar Music
All Rights Reserved. Used by Permission.

HIDE AND SEEK

Music by
THOMAS NEWMAN

© 2016 Wonderland Music Company, Inc. and Pixar Music
All Rights Reserved. Used by Permission.

QUITE A VIEW

Music by
THOMAS NEWMAN

Moderately slow, expressively

mp

Pedal ad lib.

rit.

© 2016 Wonderland Music Company, Inc. and Pixar Music
All Rights Reserved. Used by Permission.

Moderately, steadily

UNFORGETTABLE

Words and Music by
IRVING GORDON

* *Recorded a half step higher.*

Copyright © 1951 by Unforgettable Standards
Copyright Renewed
All Rights in the U.S. Administered by Sis 'N Bro Music Company c/o Carlin America, Inc.
All Rights outside the U.S. Administered by Bourne Co.
International Copyright Secured   All Rights Reserved

too.

THREE HEARTS
(End Title)

Music by
THOMAS NEWMAN

© 2016 Wonderland Music Company, Inc. and Pixar Music
All Rights Reserved. Used by Permission.

LOON TUNE

Music by
THOMAS NEWMAN

© 2016 Wonderland Music Company, Inc. and Pixar Music
All Rights Reserved. Used by Permission.

FISH WHO WANDER

Music by
THOMAS NEWMAN

© 2016 Wonderland Music Company, Inc. and Pixar Music
All Rights Reserved. Used by Permission.

Sostenuto pedal

41

WHAT A WONDERFUL WORLD

Words and Music by GEORGE DAVID WEISS
and BOB THIELE

Copyright © 1967 by Range Road Music Inc., Quartet Music and Abilene Music, Inc.
Copyright Renewed
All Rights for Quartet Music Administered by BMG Rights Management (US) LLC
All Rights for Abilene Music, Inc. Administered Worldwide by Imagem Music LLC
International Copyright Secured   All Rights Reserved
Used by Permission